turn Failure to Success

choose to CHANGE

by Grace R. Devera-Montaño

DEDICATION

To my family. I love you.

TURN FAILURE TO SUCCESS
CHOOSE TO CHANGE
Grace R. Devera-Montaño

Table of Contents

PREFACE

You want to succeed, but you do not know how. So in essence you have failed and now have a problem. If you have not admitted that yet, hopefully by the end of this section you will get to that realization. Before you dismiss this book, I implore you to hear me out and at least read the first couple pages. It will only take a few minutes of your time.

Since I asked for a few minutes of your time to preview this book, let me give you the key points up front so you can choose to put it down now or keep reading. Key points of this book are use of your *choice, time,* and *control* with their relation to failure and success. In the discussions, I will go over how to choose change using a *problem-solving tool* and provide a sample *workbook* you can use for yourself.

Many do not admit failure because they only see or focus on the surface of failure. Failure happens when expected results do not occur or are not achieved and is frequently perceived as a negative situation. My young adult son sums it up succinctly when he says *many put more value on the negative aspects of failure that it takes away from its positive aspects.* I agree. As a result, instead of thriving on failure, many try to hide failure and end up dwelling on its negative aspects. What they do not realize is that learning opportunities happen during failure. It is only when focus is shifted from the negative aspects of failure to learning opportunities that growth and success can happen.

1

In the shown diagram, the words *Failure* and *Learning* in each circle are the same type of font. The only difference is that in each circle, the font colors are changed to focus on each word. In which way are you choosing to focus?

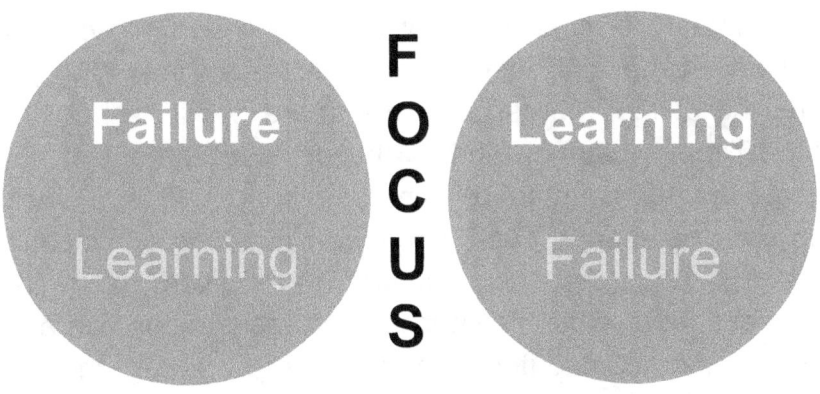

Thank you for reading this far. If you are not ready to choose to admit to your failures or problems, it is time to put this book down, stop reading, and move on to something else. However, if you are ready to choose to shift your focus from failure to learning and ready to make changes, by all means, welcome.

THERE IS NO SUCH THING AS EASY OR DIFFICULT... JUST TIME CONSUMING

There is no such thing as easy or difficult... just time-consuming. It's a phrase I often use with my children. You may disagree with me, but I believe this phrase to be true. Even the most academically challenged person can become a medical doctor if he invests time into studying and the school grants him the time he needs to become one. Time constraint hinders the accomplishment of any goal. In the example of someone becoming a medical doctor, the learner fails when he finds the educational process too time consuming and gives up. The educational institution's imposed time constraints can also be a major contributing factor to the learner giving up. Either way, the main factor to the learner's success or failure is time.

I do believe that anything can be learned. Tasks considered *easy* do not take as much time to learn or complete. Tasks considered *difficult* take longer to learn or complete. With that said, something easy or difficult comes down to how much time the person is willing to or being allowed to invest on learning or completing a task. Unfortunately, time is not infinite. Thus, a person must choose to *admit failure, learn, and change.*

Many people would say that change is difficult. What they really mean is that change is time-consuming. Change requires deviation from the usual and that takes time. Any deviation from the usual requires a person to re-learn the new way. Why learn the new way when it takes less time to do the usual? Often, the mindset of saving time blinds people from seeing the benefits of whatever change is being implemented.

As the time investment requirement increases, so does the push back for implementing change. The perception of doing things as usual becomes more desired despite of its unsuitable results. That is because many people are often in a rush to get to the next thing on their list. How many times have you heard or said the phrase *I do not have time.* It translates to *I choose to spend my time on something else.* Some say *I ran out of time*, which to me translates to *the task exceeded the amount of time I allotted for it.* If the person did not do anything at all, then the person allotted zero time. Change becomes more challenging or time-consuming as more people get involved. That is because each person controls their own time and often has their own list of things to rush to.

While in the Air Force, I had the opportunity to supervise a fellow enlisted person junior my rank. He made some minor mistakes a couple of years prior which earned him a lower performance rating compared to his peers of same rank. He felt the rating was unfair and dwelt on the negative aspects of the situation. Eventually, he shifted focus and learned from his mistakes, which improved his performance rating for the subsequent years. However, with how military promotion points are calculated, the lower ratings still weighed heavily on his chances of getting promoted. So, his negative outlook for promotion did not change.

4

I reminded him that although his performance ratings weigh high on promotion, it is only one factor and that test scores can also help him. He replied that his test scores from previous year were very inadequate and that he did not feel he will ever be good enough to score as much as what is required to get promoted. I challenged him to re-route his energy from dwelling on the negative aspects of the situation to more positive and productive efforts that are within his control. I challenged him to invest more time in studying and reading the test material since by that time, it was the only factor he had control of. He took the challenge and gave up certain activities to do just that. To make the long story short, he was the only one to get promoted amongst his peers in our organization that year.

So whatever change or improvement you are trying to make, questions to ask are: (1) *How much time am I choosing to invest in resolving this issue?* (2) *Which ones of my solutions do I have control?* *Choice* and *Control* are key elements in making change. *You* must *choose* to change focus; *choose* to invest time, and *choose* solutions within your *control*. It all comes down to *choice*.

In my subordinate's situation, he chose to make a change to focus on the positive aspects of failure. By learning from his mistakes, he earned better performance ratings the subsequent years. He also chose to stop investing time on the promotion element he no longer had control of, which were his past performance ratings. The only factor of the promotion calculation he had control of at the time was his test scores. So, he chose to invest time studying the test material. His choice garnered him a promotion.

Remember that *you only have control of yourself and not others*. Why choose to waste energy on something you do not have control of? Why choose to be frustrated as you keep trying to control others? To increase the chances of influencing an outcome you must outweigh other's control of the situation. You may be thinking that one way to do this is to make others do things your way. However, that is most likely going to be temporary because you can never have full control of others. You can keep wasting time trying to find ways to control others, or you can shift focus and invest your time wisely on things you have control of. The best way to tip the scale of influence is to focus on what you have control of.

Whether you admit it or not, you have control over your own time. Only you can choose how you spend your time. It is up to you which of your tasks get done and not done. It is up to you what to learn and not learn. It is up to you where to focus your attention. It is up to you to say *Yes* or *No* to anything. The choice is yours.

I would like to caution you with this power of controlling time. Each action has a reaction or consequence. The word *consequence* often has a negative connotation that somehow caused fear in my children when they were younger each time I mentioned the word. I reminded them that *consequence* is nothing but a result of their action. I am cautioning you in the use of controlling time because it can be very powerful. Just like you have to

6

be able to admit to failure, you have to be able to accept results or consequence of your actions, regardless if those consequences are good or bad.

PROBLEM-SOLVING TOOL - A3

There are many tools out there for problem-solving. One problem-solving tool I learned in the business environment is the A3. Many call it a problem-solving tool, but it is really more of a documentation tool. It was developed by Toyota in Japan when they decided to fit their problem-solving process into one sheet of A3-size paper. An A3-size paper is a common paper size in the Asian countries that measures 11.7 inches by 16.5 inches.

The process of finding solutions can lead to different things that take focus away from solving the problem. It can take several pages to explain the different parts of the problem-solving process. Thus, review and presentation can be overwhelming. This feeling of being overwhelmed can cause problem solvers to be distracted or give up. For ease of presentation, Toyota decided to fit the whole problem-solving process in one sheet of A3-size paper. The process in itself is basically the same as many continuous improvement process which involves planning, doing, checking, and acting, commonly referred to as PDCA, initially developed by William Deming. The difference is that the whole process is summed up in one page.

Through the years, there have been different versions of the A3 problem-solving process, but the premise remains the same, which is to fit everything on one page. By the time I started working with the A3 process, we used regular letter size paper which measures 8.5 inches by 11 inches.

So how do you fit the whole problem-solving process in one page? Boxes. Though thinking outside the box for problem solutions and many other things is helpful, each A3 process step is limited to its allotted box within the paper. Each step must fit in the box, forcing the problem solver to be succinct.

So, what does the A3 problem-solving process have to do with turning failure to succeed? The A3 process focuses on dissecting the problem and getting to the real reason the problem is occurring before coming up with solutions. Once the problem is fully understood during the dissecting process, realistic and attainable solutions are developed. Without knowing the real reason for the failure, the problem solver (that is you) is bound to repeat the same mistake because the real reason for the failure would have not been solved. Solutions that do not resolve the root cause of the problem only scratch the surface of the problem, causing failure to re-occur.

Before getting to know or dissecting a problem, you must admit to the failure first and be willing to learn from that failure. You must be able to shift focus to put less value on the negative aspects of failure and choose to put more value on its positive aspects, which is learning. Note that I use the word *choose* because it is up to you and no one else. The A3 problem-solving tool is a useful tool only if you choose to admit there is a problem and you choose to learn from it.

Once the desired solutions are chosen, the A3 process also contains steps for checking or studying the results and sustaining the solutions to maintain the desired result performance.

As you read through the next sections, use the workbook provided for your own improvement project.

A3 Sample Template

START DATE: Be Specific END DATE: Be Specific	TITLE: 5-10 WORDS	OWNER: Your Name
1. CLARIFY THE PROBLEM	3. DETERMINE PROBLEM ROOT CAUSES	5. CHOSEN SOLUTIONS
2. WHAT ARE THE GAPS?		6. FOLLOW-UP
	4. PRIORITIZE SOLUTIONS	
3. DESIRED RESULTS		6. SUSTAINMENT PLAN

GETTING TO KNOW THE PROBLEM

If you are still reading, then you are committed to making a change, so let's go!

The first part of change is to choose for yourself to make a change. It is important to decide to choose to make the change on your own and not because others told you to do it. Ownership is an important aspect of change. If you do not own the problem, in essence you are putting the blame for the problem on someone or something else. By doing that, you are admitting to not having control of the problem or situation. As previously mentioned, you should only work on something within your control. Otherwise, your solutions may be futile. Besides, if you do not take ownership by choosing for yourself, then the problem belongs to someone else. In essence, you do not have a problem. So why solve someone else's problem?

Once you have chosen for yourself to make the change, the next step is to choose to admit failure. By doing so, you are admitting that a problem exists. Again, why make a change if there is no problem. Some may say *I don't really have a problem. I just want to improve.* Well, you can call it whatever you want, but the way I see it, anything that you would like to change or have a question on is in essence a problem. A problem does not have to be big. It can vary from small inquiries for yourself like deciding on what snack to eat to life-changing issues like a career change.

Choosing for yourself to make a change and admitting to the failure are key to problem-solving and thus are key to using the A3 problem-solving tool successfully. Skipping these steps result to not having the need for this problem-solving tool because *you* do not have a problem to solve. It is either the problem belongs to someone else, or you did not fail so there is no problem.

In getting to know the problem, it is important to clarify the problem, determine what is missing or gaps, decide on the desired result(s), and find the root cause(s) of the problem. It is in this group of steps that a problem is dissected for better understanding in order to get to the real reason the problem is occurring.

Clarify The Problem

To solve any problem, it is important to clearly define the problem. Otherwise, you could end up with solutions that do not apply to the problem and still be stuck with the same dilemma. To help with clarifying the problem, answer the questions below.

1. What is the perceived problem?
2. When did the problem start?
3. How much time do I want to invest in this problem?
4. Where is the problem happening?
5. Who or what is the problem affecting?
6. Why is it important to solve this problem?
7. What happens if the problem continues?

Keep your answers short and as specific as possible. The answers to these questions will have to fit into the box within the A3 paper, or in most current cases, a letter size paper. To better focus on solutions, use the A3 problem-solving tool for one problem at a time.

What Are The Gaps?

Once the problem is clarified, it's time to start dissecting it to gain further clarification. Is it a real problem or is it just a perceived problem? If there really is a problem, then there should be a gap between the ideal situation and current situation. It is also important to ask whether the ideal situation is realistic to achieve. If not, what should be the realistic situation and is there a gap between that and the current situation? Measure these gaps and record them. Measurements are vital to having tangible results. Tangible results aid in understanding the failure or success of an improvement project.

It is also important to know the process that led to the current situation. Often times, a formal process exists but not followed, resulting to the problem. If there is no formal process, outline the sequence of events that lead to the current situation. Writing out the process or sequence of events helps clarify necessary, unnecessary, and missing steps.

Below are helpful questions to determine the gap.

1. What is the ideal situation?
2. Is the ideal situation realistic?

3. If ideal situation is not realistic, what is considered realistic situation?
4. What is the current situation?
5. What is the gap between ideal and current situation?
6. What is the gap between realistic and current situation?
7. Is there a formal process or written instruction for the sequence of events leading to the desired results?
8. Is the formal process or written instructions being followed?
9. If written instructions are not being followed, which steps are non-compliant (being skipped or not followed)?

Show the gaps and process visually using a graph and process map. Graphs and process maps are helpful in identifying gaps. Measuring and graphing the gap help better visualize the problem. Drawing and visualizing the process or sequence of events help identify the steps not being followed, missing steps that should be in place, or other gaps in the process. Provided are sample visualizations of a problem.

The graph sample shows the gap between a person's goal to watch no more than five hours of television each week and current situation where the person is watching 30 hours of television in one week. Through this visualization, the problem solver can see when the problem started.

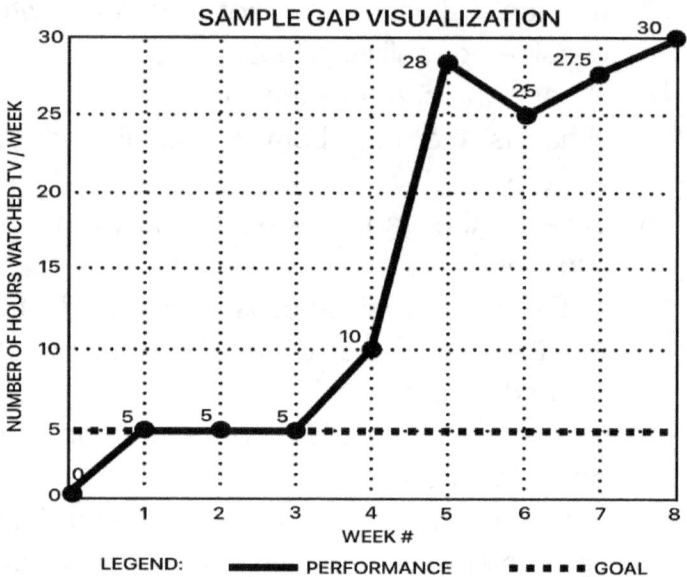

SAMPLE GAP VISUALIZATION

Chart showing NUMBER OF HOURS WATCHED TV / WEEK (y-axis, 0 to 30) versus WEEK # (x-axis, 1 to 8)

Data points: Week 0: 0, Week 1: 5, Week 2: 5, Week 3: 5, Week 4: 10, Week 5: 28, Week 6: 25, Week 7: 27.5, Week 8: 30

LEGEND: —— PERFORMANCE ▪▪▪▪ GOAL

The process map sample shows the sequence of events that lead to the problem solver's challenge of watching more than five hours of television per week. In a process map, beginning and ending steps are typically represented by a circle; decisions are represented by a diamond; and steps in the process that do not require decisions are represented by rectangles. Arrows connect the elements to show how the sequence of events flows. After drawing out the process map, it helps to highlight the problem areas with red font or an X.

PROCESS MAP SAMPLE

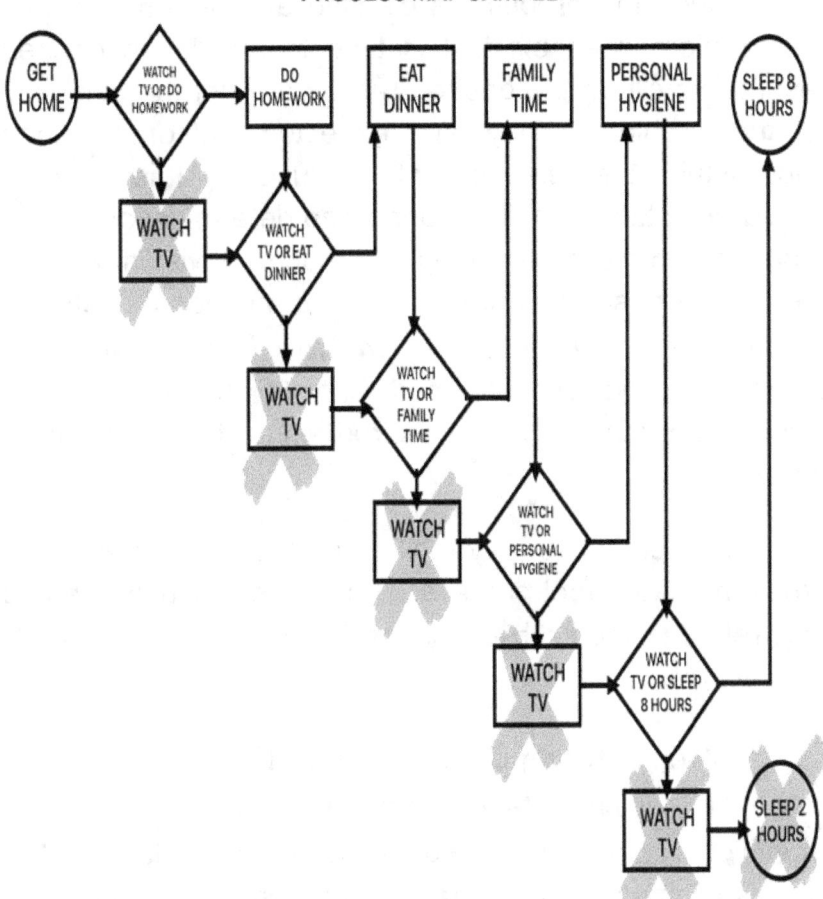

Desired Results

Once the problem is clarified and determined that the problem does exist, it is time to decide on desired results. Note that the desired results are not the solutions to the problem. They are expected outcomes upon successful implementation of the solution(s). It is the ideal or realistic state identified during gap determination. In the problem sample of watching too much television weekly, the problem solver chose to make his ideal state as *watching television no more than five hours a week*. To prevent getting overwhelmed and to better focus on solutions, narrow down the desired results to no more than three.

Remember to only tackle one problem for each A3 problem-solving tool process. The desired result(s) should only relate to the problem defined in the first step, *Clarify the Problem*.

When deciding on desired results, use the *SMART* acronym which stands for *Specific, Measurable, Achievable, Relevant,* and *Time-related*. Having the criteria of specific, measurable, and achievable make the result(s) tangible or realistic. As mentioned earlier, tangible results aid in understanding failure or success of an improvement project. Making it measurable helps the problem solver recognize any improvement or decrement from baseline performance or from the time change initiative was started. To better focus on making results achievable, limit the desired results to no more than three.

Remember that desired results are the outcome(s), not solutions.

Relevancy of the result can be subjective to the situation. It just means that the results must have an important effect or impact to the problem solver. In a business change initiative, the results must have an impact to the business or to the people running the business. The first step *Clarify the Problem* specifies what the problem is affecting. That same relevancy should be the same for this step, *Desired Results.*

Although I said earlier that there is no such thing as easy or difficult, just time consuming, desired results should have an estimated completion time. Anything can be learned, but let's face it, no one has infinite amount of time. That is why it is important to decide from the very beginning how much time to invest and how many tasks to work on prior to tackling any challenge.

One misconception is that doing more equals productivity. My young adult daughter summed it up in her observation that people often connect their value with productivity or getting things done, which often translates to doing more, resulting to failed multi-tasking. I liken people to computers. Just like computers run out of memory and freezes when executing several programs, people also run out of energy when overtasked, resulting in failure.

That does not mean succumbing to the first failure or that any knowledge from failure gets wasted.

Remember, failure is a key to success because that is where learning happens.

Ask these questions for each desired result to ensure each one is *SMART*.

1. Is the desired result *Specific*?
2. Is the desired result *Measurable*?
3. Is the desired result *Achievable*?
4. Is the desired result *Relevant*?
5. Is the desired result *Time-related*?

Use the table template below to record desired results.

METRIC	CURRENT METRIC (DATE)	DESIRED METRIC STATE	ESTIMATED COMPLETE DATE	RELEVANT TO WHO?	STATUS

Determine Problem Root Causes

Some problem solvers dive in right away to creating solutions without determining root causes. Doing this, results to higher chances of creating irrelevant solutions that may not solve the problem.

I used to tell my children that they cannot eat a whole steak in one bite. The steak needs to be cut into smaller pieces. That is similar to solving problems. A problem can sometimes seem so big that it becomes overwhelming to start solving it. That is why it is important to dissect a problem into smaller ones. This can be done through root cause analysis.

Root cause analysis uses the process of deductive reasoning to arrive to a more specific cause of the problem. You can liken solving root causes to eliminating weeds on your lawn. Some try to eliminate weeds on their lawn with a mower. However, by doing that, only the top part of the weeds is eliminated. The weeds' roots are still alive and in a few days they will be back. Additionally, in the process of mowing, parts of the weeds are scattered throughout the lawn to germinate, causing more weeds. You can try weed killer solutions, but most often times the weed killer solution also kills the grass on your lawn. The most effective way is to manually dig the weeds out to include the roots and dispose of them in the garbage.

While I was in the military, one problem our organization had to deal with was for new airmen to pass their Career Development Course (CDC) test. Airmen who fail their tests are normally reprimanded and required to have supervised study time at work during off-duty hours. Although supervised, the airmen studied on their own quietly in one room with a group of airmen. That way, only one supervisor needed to be present. The aim was to make sure the airmen allotted time to studying. On the surface, it seems like a solution that makes sense, but it does not work for everyone. Though it seems helpful, the supervised study time only scratched the surface of the true problem. Almost all of them failed the practice test. Even after passing their practice test, some still failed their official CDC test a second time and some barely passed.

Root causes of problems are the real reasons problems are occurring. A series of interviews with individual airmen and with the help of the Base Education Center, we eventually determined the root causes or real reasons our airmen failed their CDC test. Each airman's reason for failing was unique. Root causes varied, such as allotted study time, learning deficiency, language barrier, and motivation. Once root causes were recognized, unique solutions were created such as offering lessons on effective study skills, one on one study help, and positive reinforcements in the form of rewards like a three-day pass for achieving a score of 90% or higher.

Two tools I like using for root cause analysis are the *Ishikawa Diagram*, also known as the *Fishbone Analysis* and the *Five Why's Analysis.*

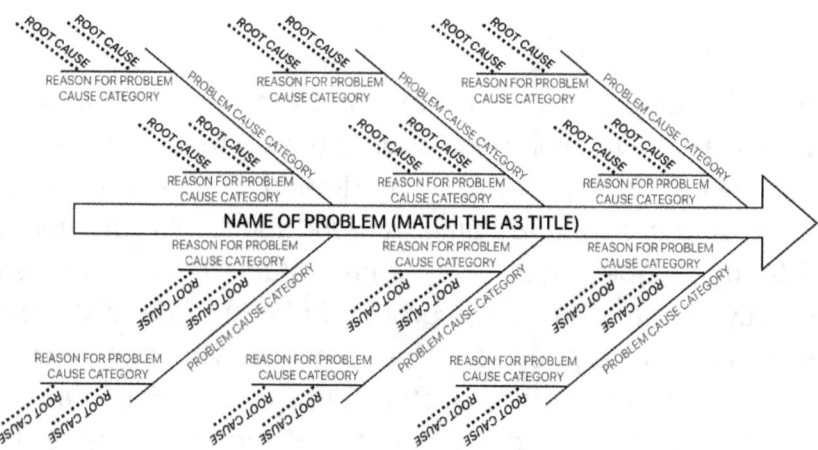

Above is an example of a *Fishbone Analysis*. In Fishbone Analysis, the name of the problem is placed on the center arrow. Branches or fishbones are then placed on the arrow signifying the different categories of problem causes. Common main categories I like to use are: People, Resources, Processes or Methods, Policies, Measurement, and Environment. Branches are then placed on each main branch specifying the reason that main category is a problem cause. Additional branches are added to the secondary branches further specifying why the secondary branch is a problem cause.

This process can be repeated several times. It is important to remember that each branch level is answering the question *Why?* of the previous branch level, and not the main problem. The latter will keep the questioning at the same branch level. Remember that the purpose of the branch levels is to deduce the reasoning to the root cause. Each level of branches is a sub-cause of the previous branch. The last level of branches for each main branch contains the root causes. In the sample Fishbone diagram previously shown, the root cause branches have dotted lines and have darker texts. Using the sample diagram, there are 24 root causes to that specific problem, assuming there are no duplicates.

Root causes often show up in more than one category causing duplicates, and that is acceptable. It only means that those root causes affect or impact multiple problem cause categories. For example, you can have ten problems cause categories and end up with one root cause. Note that it is best to narrow down the last level root causes to ten or less to better focus on solutions.

The second root cause analysis tool I like using is the *Five Why's Analysis*. This tool is similar to the Fishbone Analysis tool except it specifies to use the question *Why?* five times. Similar to the Fishbone Analysis, come up with five to six categories of contributing factors the problem exists. Using categories increase the chances of addressing applicable causes contributing to the problem, thus resulting to more effective root cause analysis.

Work on each category one at a time by answering the question *Why?* five times. The fifth reason for each category is a root cause. Similar to the Fishbone Analysis, remember that each *Why?* level is answering the question *Why?* of the previous branch, and not of the main problem. Otherwise, the reasoning would remain in the same level *Why?* The purpose of asking the question *Why?* five times is to deduce the problem to the root cause. In the diagram shown, the fifth reason is printed darker to signify as root cause. Repeat this process for each reason category.

PROBLEM	
#1 WHY?	REASON 1
#2 WHY?	REASON 2
#3 WHY?	REASON 3
#4 WHY?	REASON 4
#5 WHY?	**REASON 5 - ROOT CAUSE**

Similar to the Fishbone Analysis, duplicate root causes often emerge in different categories and that is acceptable. Duplicate root causes mean that common issue exists for the different problem cause categories. That can be a good thing because you can focus your solution to that common issue that affects a wider scope of the problem. Sometimes, the root cause for all categories ends up being the same, resulting in one root cause to solve.

In some cases, the root cause for one problem cause category ends up in the middle of another problem cause category. When that happens, that particular root cause cancels and the *Why?* questioning continues in the middle of the other problem cause category. See below for illustration. In the sample shown, even though there are three problem cause categories, there is only one root cause.

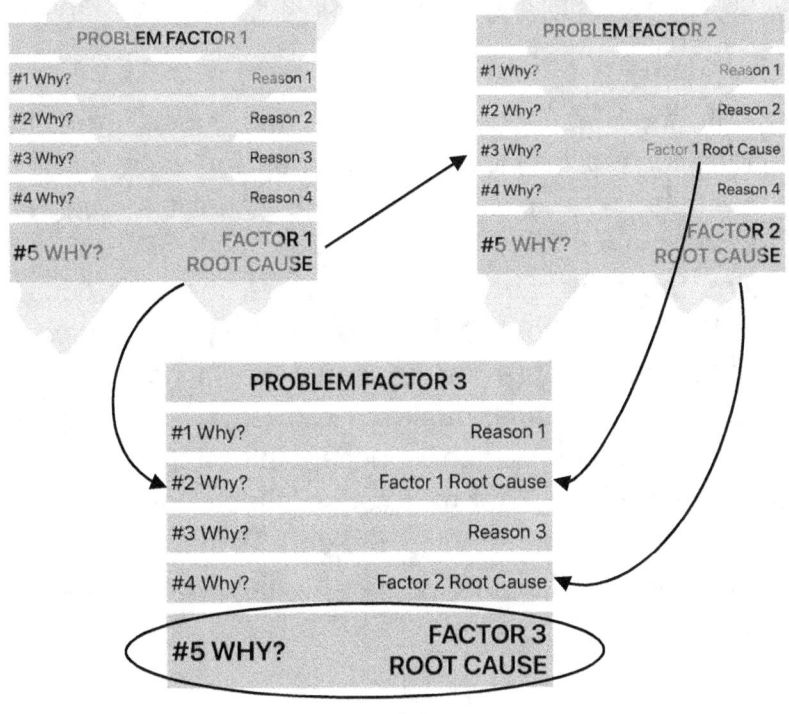

SOLUTIONS AND IMPLEMENTATION

Now that you have gotten to know the problem and dissected it, it is time to develop solutions. As mentioned earlier, it is best to create solutions for the root cause(s) of the problem because root causes are the real reason for the problem. Just like weeds on your lawn, you would want to eliminate the roots to prevent them from coming back.

Develop Solutions

Like the desired results, effective solutions are *SMART* — *Specific, Measurable, Achievable, Relevant, Time-related*. In developing solutions, refer back to the root cause analysis and develop solutions for the identified root causes.

If the Fishbone Analysis was used, develop solutions for the last level of branches for each problem cause category. In the Fishbone Analysis diagram provided as an example, the last level of branches contains the root causes. Assuming all the root causes entered are different, which is unlikely, the sample Fishbone Analysis previously shown would have 24 root causes. In most cases, duplicate root causes emerge for multiple categories, which is acceptable. The more root cause categories a final root cause affects the higher its impact on the actual change project. To better focus on finding solutions, it is best to narrow final root causes to ten or less.

If the Five Why's tool was used, develop solutions for the fifth reason for each category. The answer to the fifth *Why?* is considered a root cause. Remember to have at least five problem cause categories and conduct the Five Why's test for each. Each problem cause category will result to a root cause. Similar to the Fishbone Analysis, duplicate root causes may show up in different categories. If lucky, there will only be one root cause for all five problem cause categories.

To assist with the next step of prioritizing solutions, it is helpful to determine the estimated amount of impact each solution will have on the problem. It is also helpful to determine the estimated amount of effort each solution will require for implementation. Below is a sample table to use during solution development.

#	Root Causes (Not Prioritized)	SMART Solution A	SMART Solution B (Optional)	SMART Solution C (Optional)
1		1A SMART: Yes No Impact: Low Med Hi Effort: Low Med Hi	1B SMART: Yes No Impact: Low Med Hi Effort: Low Med Hi	1C SMART: Yes No Impact: Low Med Hi Effort: Low Med Hi
2		2A SMART: Yes No Impact: Low Med Hi Effort: Low Med Hi	2B SMART: Yes No Impact: Low Med Hi Effort: Low Med Hi	2C SMART: Yes No Impact: Low Med Hi Effort: Low Med Hi

Prioritize Solutions

Once solutions have been developed for root causes, it is time to start prioritizing them. When considering effort needed for implementation, remember to factor in the availability of resources such as people, funds, and time. The more resources needed to implement, the higher the effort needed for implementation. It is also important to consider which of these resources are within your control. Anything outside your control is most likely to result in more effort during implementation. In considering time as a factor for effort, remember that there is no such thing as easy or difficult, just time consuming. Refer back to the first step of *Clarify the Problem* and third step, *Desired Results*. Take note of the time constraint allotted for this initiative and factor them into the prioritization process.

Prioritize the list of developed solutions using the *Prioritization Matrix*. The Prioritization Matrix is in essence a graph. The *Y axis* or vertical axis of the graph measures the impact of a solution. The *X axis* or horizontal axis of the graph measures the amount of effort needed to implement the solution. Solutions requiring the lowest effort to implement but with high impact are ideal solutions while solutions requiring the highest effort to implement but lowest impact are less suitable solutions.

For simplification, the graph is divided into four quadrants. The top left quadrant is for solutions that require less effort to implement but have high impact. These solutions are considered acceptable and recommended to have high priority for implementation. They are sometimes coined as *low hanging fruits* because like low hanging fruits that can easily be picked and enjoyed, these solutions can easily be implemented and have high impact.

The lower left quadrant is for solutions that require less effort to implement and have low impact. These solutions are less suitable because of their low impact. The bottom right quadrant is for solutions that require high effort to implement but less impact. These solutions are considered the least suitable or in some cases unsuitable. Solutions in this quadrant are often placed as low priority for implementation. The top right quadrant is for solutions that require high effort for implementation and have high impact. In some cases, solutions in this quadrant require business case analysis to determine if the impact is high enough to create a return on investment. In other words, are the results worth the work?

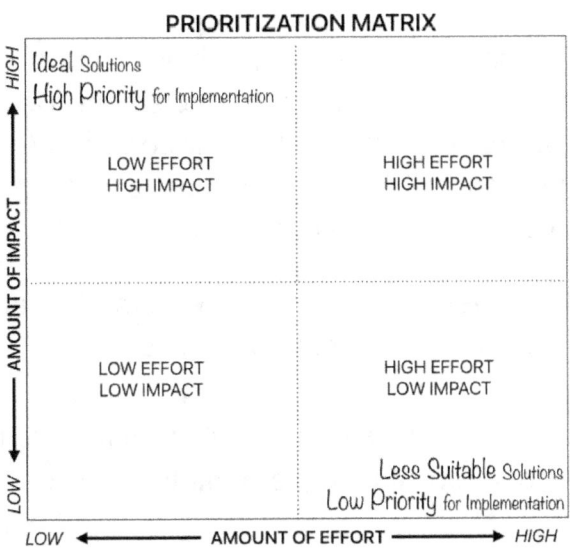

PRIORITIZATION MATRIX

Once all the solutions are placed on the Prioritization Matrix, re-list the solutions in priority order.

Priority	Prioritized SMART Solutions	Estimated Completion Date	Root Cause(s) Affected
1			
2			
3			
4			
5			

Chosen Solutions

Now that the developed solutions are prioritized, it is time to choose which ones to implement. Be cognizant of your resources in relation to your solutions (i.e. people, funds, time, etc.). These resources should have been factored in during prioritization.

To prevent getting overwhelmed, recommend choosing solutions that can be implemented within the time constraints established during *Clarify the Problem* and *Desired Results* steps. It also helps to have the resources needed for implementation to be available and/or within your control. Keep the other solutions on the list to work on later.

Remember that you are like a computer that can shut down when overtasked. Multi-tasking and doing more do not necessarily equate to productivity. To better focus on results, narrow down your chosen solutions to ten or less. If you are doing this as a personal project, start with one to five solutions since you will most likely be the only one doing all the work.

Below is a sample table template to list SMART solutions.

CHOSEN SOLUTIONS	START DATE	ESTIMATED COMPLETION DATE	POINT OF CONTACT	STATUS / COMMENTS

FOLLOW-UP

Once solution implementation starts, it is important to follow-up periodically to ensure things are going the way they are supposed to. Monitor the results of the chosen solutions and how they are impacting the desired results. Check the status at least monthly for both solutions and desired results. Check them weekly if the estimated completion time allotted during *Desired Results* step is within three months or less of the start date. Remember to include the date each time a status or comment is entered.

As a review, below are the tables for *Desired Results* and *Chosen Solutions* that require updates periodically.

METRIC / MEASURE	CURRENT STATE MEASUREMENT (DATE)	DESIRED STATE MEASUREMENT	ESTIMATED COMPLETION DATE	WHO IS THIS RELEVANT TO?	STATUS / COMMENTS

CHOSEN SOLUTIONS	START DATE	ESTIMATED COMPLETION DATE	POINT OF CONTACT	STATUS / COMMENTS

Monitoring is important so that you will know whether an adjustment to the chosen solutions is needed.

To stay within the time constraints, use the 25% rule for re-assessment. If the initiative is not progressing within the 25% of the time allotted for completion, conduct a re-assessment. To conduct a re-assessment, re-accomplish the following three steps: *Determine Problem Root Causes, Prioritize Solutions,* and *Chosen Solutions.*

In monitoring the status of solutions and desired results, it helps to visualize the progress of the desired results. Measure and document the progress of desired results each time you conduct a follow-up. Visualize the progress by using the graph provided in the second step, *What are the Gaps?* Visualize the progress for each desired result.

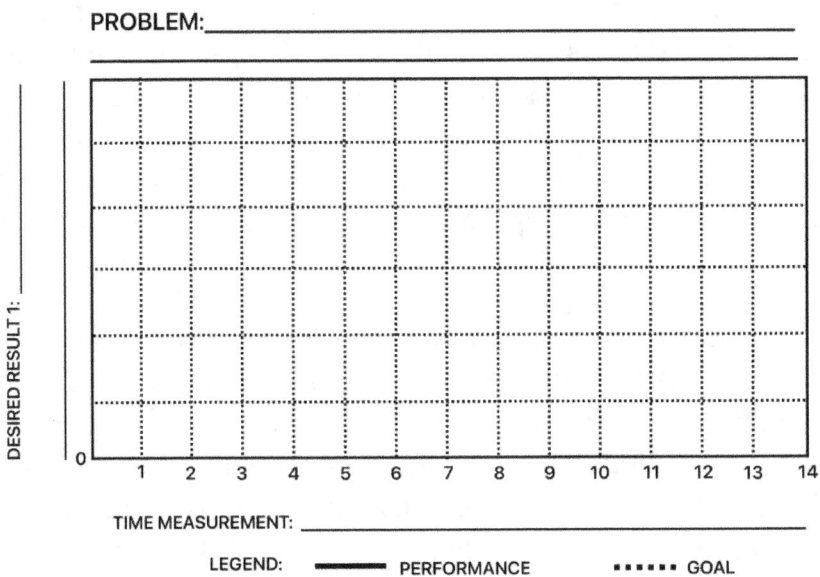

SUSTAINMENT

It is important to have a sustainment plan once the desired results are achieved to ensure that the problem does not return. Part of sustainment is documentation of what was done. It is essential to document what was done not only for historical purposes but also for continuity purposes. Documentation for continuity purposes is especially important in a business environment because of possible employee turnover. Part of documentation is developing written processes for others to follow. Standardizing processes helps with replicability of solutions and achievement of consistent results.

If completing this journey for personal reasons, documentation would be accomplished through journaling. Documentation is just as important for personal reasons as it is in a business environment. Having something written down to refer back to, helps with remembering the steps that need to be taken to continue implementing the solutions. It also helps with mindfulness and establishing habits.

Continue to monitor results for solution implementation and their impact on the desired results. Continued monitoring is vital to ensure continued solution implementation. Monitoring reinforces implementation until it becomes a standard practice within the organization or in personal case, a habit. Conduct a follow-up once a month for the first six months, then quarterly for the next year, and at least every six months thereafter.

If the time constraint established in *Desired Results* step is within three months, adjust the follow-up time to every week until desired results are achieved. After desired results are achieved, conduct a follow-up every month for six months. Then conduct the subsequent follow-ups quarterly for a year. By then, hopefully, the implemented solutions will become a standard practice or a habit for personal cases. Once that happens, sustainment still needs to occur to ensure the installed solutions continue to function. So, by then, conduct the follow-ups at least every six months.

Below are sample templates to use for the periodic follow-up during the sustainment step.

DESIRED RESULTS CHECK-UP	MO1	MO2	MO3	MO4	MO5	MO6	YR1 QTR1	YR1 QTR2	YR1 QTR3	YR1 QTR4	YR2 MO6	YR2 MO12	YR3 MO6	YR3 MO12

CHOSEN SOLUTIONS CHECK-UP	MO1	MO2	MO3	MO4	MO5	MO6	YR1 QTR1	YR1 QTR2	YR1 QTR3	YR1 QTR4	YR2 MO6	YR2 MO12	YR3 MO6	YR3 MO12

As part of sustainment, it is also important to continue updating the visualization tools for each desired results for continued monitoring. The visualization tool can show trends that can open further improvement projects at a future date.

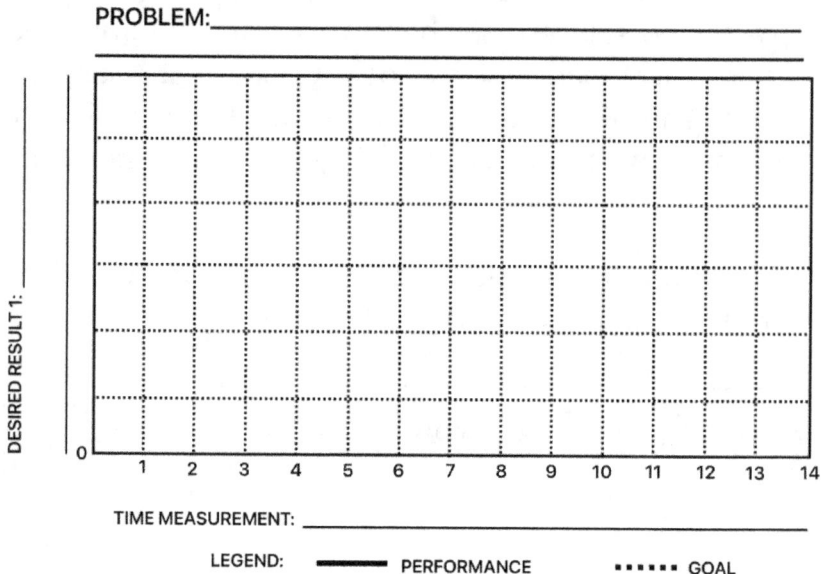

PROBLEM:_____

DESIRED RESULT 1: _____

TIME MEASUREMENT: _____

LEGEND: ━━━ PERFORMANCE ▪▪▪▪▪ GOAL

AFTERWORD

Thank you for reading through this short book. I hope that you have learned something or at least got a refresher on problem solving. I say refresher because it is nothing new. One way or another someone has written about it or most likely told you about it. Some just break it down a little bit more than others so that they are more understandable. Some just speaks better to you and your senses. Whatever the case may be, I hope it helps.

The first takeaway I would like to emphasize is that a key to success is *choice*. Everything is up to you. You have to choose to succeed. You have to choose to admit failure and choose to make a change. The concepts outlined here will not work unless you choose to admit to failing and having a problem, because otherwise, there is no problem to solve. You have to choose to focus on the positive aspects of failure which is learning. After all. It is through failure that learning happens. By making a choice, you are taking ownership of the situation, thus gaining *control*, which is the second takeaway.

You only have control of your own actions. As much as you may want to control others, the fact remains that each person has their own will to control. You can only control yourself. You can choose to waste time trying to control others and be frustrated, or you can choose to control your time. That leads to the third takeaway, *time*.

There is no such thing as easy or difficult... only time-consuming. Without time constraints, you can learn anything. Unfortunately, life often does not afford everyone to have enough time to do everything. No one has infinite time to accomplish a task. That leads back to the first takeaway of choice. You have to make a choice on how you want to spend your time. You must choose what to focus on. *You choose*.

The A3 problem-solving tool is summarized below for your convenience. The next pages are provided for you as a workbook to make a change. Good luck and stay focused.

START DATE: Be specific END DATE: Be specific	TITLE: 5-10 WORDS	OWNER: Your Name

1. CLARIFY THE PROBLEM
· What is the perceived problem?
· When did the problem start?
· How much time do I want to invest in this problem-solving process?
  · Recommend 6-12 months or less.
· Where is the problem happening?
· Who or what is the problem affecting?
· Why is it important to solve this problem?
· What happens if the problem continues?
	4. DETERMINE PROBLEM ROOT CAUSES
	· *Choose one tool below.*
	  · Five Whys
	    · List five to six problem causes.
	    · Ask "Why" 5x for each problem cause.
	    · Each 5th answer is a root cause.
	  · Fish Bone Diagram
	    · List six problem cause categories.
	    · On the next branch, list why the previous branch is considered a problem.
		6. CHOSEN SOLUTIONS
		· Pick the solution you would like to implement from Box 5.
		· Specify start date, expected completion date, and status for each solution.
		· Remain consistent by choosing solutions that can be achieved by the date entered in Box 3.

2. WHAT ARE THE GAPS?
· Describe the gaps.
  · What is the ideal state? Is it realistic?
  · What is the realistic state?
  · What is the current state?
  · What are the gaps between ideal vs realistic vs current state?
· Describe the process in getting to current state.
  · Is there a process? Is it being followed?
  · If the process is not being followed, what steps are not being followed?
· Graph the gaps and process.
	5. PRIORITIZE SOLUTIONS
	· *Choose one tool from Box 4 and write SMART solutions for each root cause.*
	  · Fish Bone Diagram
	    · Write solutions for last branches.
	  · Five Whys
	    · Write solutions for each 5th answer.
	· *SMART Solutions*
	  · Specific, Measurable, Achievable, Relevant, Time-Related
	· *Prioritize Solutions*
	  · Use the prioritization matrix.
	  · Re-list solutions in priority order based on the results from the prioritization matrix.
		7. FOLLOW-UP
		· Monitor results of solutions & desired results.
		· Check status at least monthly. Check weekly if Box 3 target date is within 3 months or less.
		· Enter the date for each status/comment entry
		· Follow 20% rule. Divide allotted time in Box 1 by 5. If not progressing by that time, conduct a re-assessment by re-doing Boxes 4-6.
		
		8. SUSTAINMENT PLAN
		· Set-up *written* processes (habits if using for personal improvement) that includes Box 6 solutions.
		· Monitor results of solutions & desired results.
		  · Check status monthly the first 6 months, then quarterly for a year, then every 6 months thereafter.

3. DESIRED RESULTS · List three SMART results. · SMART - Specific, Measurable, Achievable, Relevant, Time-Related · Recommended completion: 6-12 months or less · Be consistent with the amount of time allotted in Box 1.		

LARGER PICTURES OF A3 BOXES

TITLE: 5-10 WORDS

START DATE: Be specific
END DATE: Be specific

OWNER: Your Name

1. CLARIFY THE PROBLEM
- *What is the perceived problem?*
- *When did the problem start?*
- *How much time do I want to invest in this problem-solving process?*
  - *Recommend 6-12 months or less.*
- *Where is the problem happening?*
- *Who or what is the problem affecting?*
- *Why is it important to solve this problem?*
- *What happens if the problem continues?*

2. WHAT ARE THE GAPS?
- *Describe the gaps.*
  - *What is the ideal state? Is it realistic?*
  - *What is the realistic state?*
  - *What is the current state?*
  - *What are the gaps between ideal vs realistic vs current state?*
- *Describe the process in getting to current state.*
  - *Is there a process? Is it being followed?*
  - *If the process is not being followed, what steps are not being followed?*
- *Graph the gaps and process.*

3. DESIRED RESULTS
- *List three SMART results.*
- *SMART - Specific, Measurable, Achievable, Relevant, Time-Related*
- *Recommended completion: 6-12 months or less*
- *Be consistent with the amount of time allotted in Box 1.*

METRIC / MEASURE	CURRENT STATE MEASUREMENT (DATE)	DESIRED STATE MEASUREMENT	ESTIMATED COMPLETION DATE	WHO IS THIS RELEVANT TO?	STATUS / COMMENTS

4. DETERMINE PROBLEM ROOT CAUSES
- ***Choose one tool below.***
  - *Five Why's*
    - *List five to six problem causes.*
    - *Ask "Why" 5x for each problem cause.*
    - *Each 5th answer is a root cause.*
  - *Fish Bone Diagram*
    - *List six problem cause categories.*
    - *On the next branch, list why the previous branch is considered a problem.*

NAME OF PROBLEM (MATCH THE A3 TITLE)

5. PRIORITIZE SOLUTIONS

- *Choose one tool from Box 4 and write SMART solutions for each root cause.*
  - *Fish Bone Diagram*
    - *Write solutions for last branches.*
  - *Five Why's*
    - *Write solutions for each 5th answer.*
- *SMART Solutions*
  - *Specific, Measurable, Achievable, Relevant, Time-Related*
- *Prioritize Solutions*
  - *Use the prioritization matrix.*
  - *Re-list solutions in priority order based on the results from the prioritization matrix.*

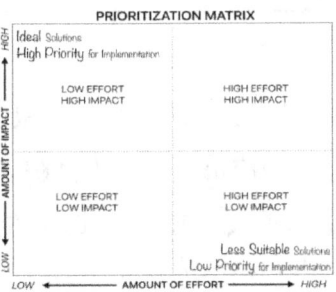

PRIORITIZATION MATRIX

6. CHOSEN SOLUTIONS

- *Pick the solution you would like to implement from Box 5.*
- *Specify start date, expected completion date, and status for each solution.*
- *Remain consistent by choosing solutions that can be achieved by the date entered in Box 3.*

CHOSEN SOLUTIONS	START DATE	ESTIMATED COMPLETION DATE	POINT OF CONTACT	STATUS / COMMENTS

7. FOLLOW-UP

- *Monitor results of solutions & desired results.*
- *Check status at least monthly. Check weekly if Box 3 target date is within 3 months or less.*
- *Enter the date for each status/comment entry.*
- *Follow 20% rule. Divide allotted time in Box 1 by 5. If not progressing by that time, conduct a re-assessment by re-doing Boxes 4-6.*

8. SUSTAINMENT PLAN

- Set-up **written** processes (habits if using for personal improvement) that includes Box 6 solutions.
- Monitor results of solutions & desired results.
  - Check status monthly the first 6 months, then quarterly for a year, then every 6 months thereafter.

DESIRED RESULTS CHECK-UP	MO1	MO2	MO3	MO4	MO5	MO6	YR1 QTR1	YR1 QTR2	YR1 QTR3	YR1 QTR4	YR2 MO6	YR2 MO12	YR3 MO6	YR3 MO12

CHOSEN SOLUTIONS CHECK-UP	MO1	MO2	MO3	MO4	MO5	MO6	YR1 QTR1	YR1 QTR2	YR1 QTR3	YR1 QTR4	YR2 MO6	YR2 MO12	YR3 MO6	YR3 MO12

turn Failure to Success

choose to CHANGE

by Grace R. Devera-Montaño

THE WORKBOOK

STEP 1: CLARIFY THE PROBLEM

PROBLEM TITLE:

What is the perceived problem?

When did the problem start?

How much time do I want to invest?

Number of Years: _____ Number of Days: _____

Number of Months: _____ Number of Hours: _____

Number of Weeks: _____ Number of Minutes: _____

When did the problem Start? *Be as specific as possible.*

Where is the problem happening?

Who or what is the problem affecting?

Why is it important to solve this problem?

What happens if the problem continues?

STEP 2: WHAT ARE THE GAPS?

PROBLEM TITLE:

What is the ideal state or situation? *This is not the solution, but rather the ideal end result. Write in a way that it can be measured.*

Is the ideal situation realistic? YES   NO

If ideal situation is not realistic, what is considered realistic?

What is the current situation? *Write in a way that it can be measured.*

What is the gap between ideal and current situation? *Write in a way that it can be measured.*

What is the gap between realistic and current situation? *Write in a way that it can be measured.*

Is there a formal process or written instructions for sequence of events? YES NO	**Is the formal process or written instructions being followed?** YES NO
If formal process is not being followed, which steps are being skipped?	
Show visualization of the gaps? *See below for visualization template.*	**Show visualization of process gaps?** *See below for visualization template.*

45

Gap Visualization:

- Write a short title for the problem on top of the graph.
- On the left side, write down the item you are measuring after the word "PERFORMANCE".
- After the number "0", fill in the number scale upwards of how you want to measure your performance.
  - Be consistent with number increments.
- Towards the bottom of the graph, write down the type of time measurement you are using.
  - Time: minutes, hours, days, weeks, months, years.
  - Change the number scale as needed but be consistent.
- On the graph itself, plot your performance.
  - Use a solid line for current performance and a dotted line for the goal.
- Create a graph for each desired result.

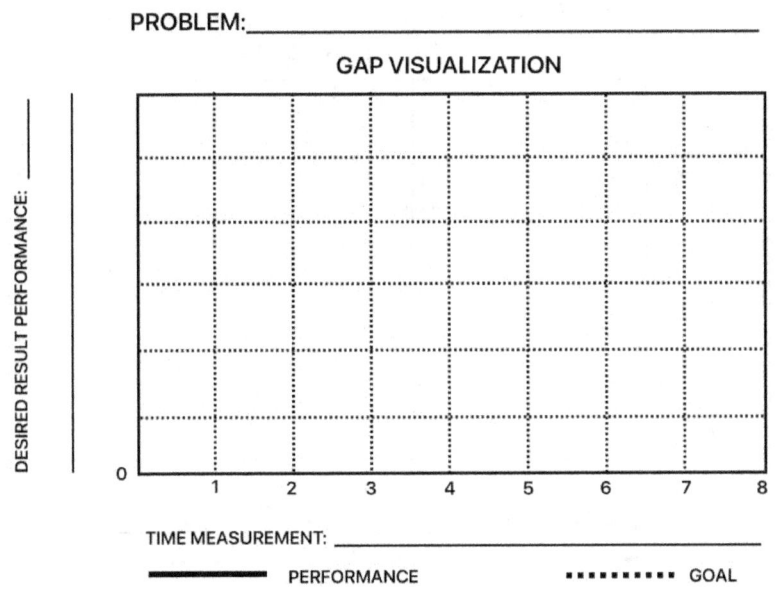

PROBLEM:_____

GAP VISUALIZATION

DESIRED RESULT PERFORMANCE: _____

TIME MEASUREMENT: _____

━━━━ PERFORMANCE   ▪▪▪▪▪▪▪▪▪ GOAL

Gap Visualization (Continued)

PROBLEM:_____

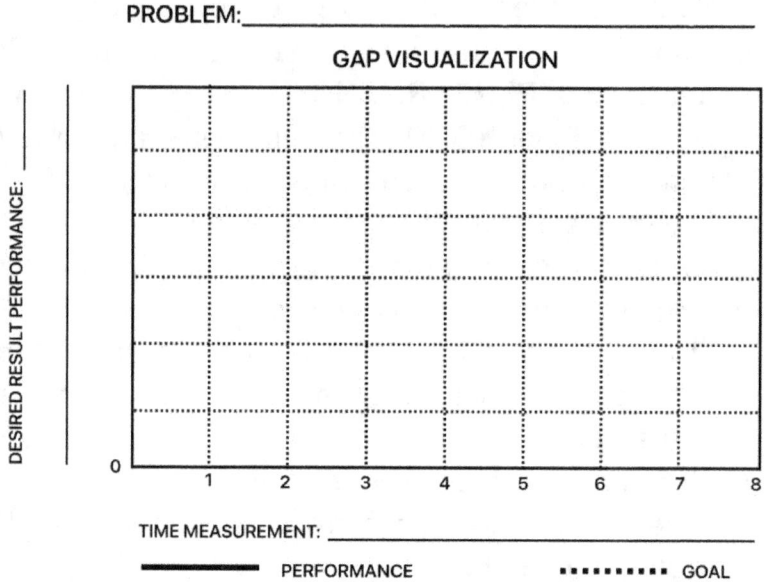

PROBLEM:_____

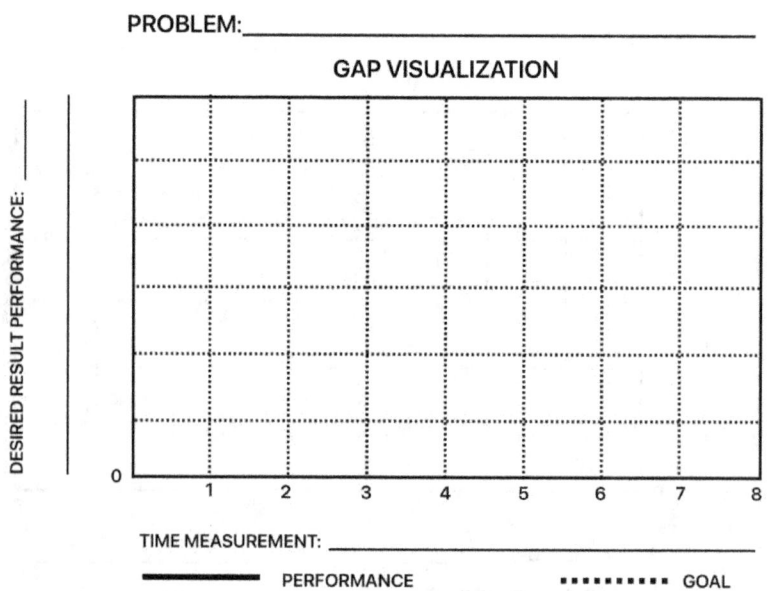

Process Map Gap Visualization:

- Use the space on the next page to draw your process to visualize the problem. See process map sample below and in *What Are the Gaps?* step for reference.
  - Use circle shape for start and end of the process.
    - The start circle leads *to* one step – a rectangle or a diamond shape.
    - The end circle can lead *from* several steps.
  - Use rectangle shape for process steps that do not require a decision.
    - Each rectangle step leads to one step – another rectangle, a diamond, or a circle shape.
  - Use diamond shape for process steps requiring decisions.
    - Each corner of the diamond signifies a decision that can lead to a different step.
    - At least two corners must lead to another shape to use the diamond shape; otherwise use a rectangle or circle.
    - Most common choice decisions are *Yes* or *No*.
- Mark process step(s) that are problematic or being skipped with an X.
- Use arrows to connect elements.

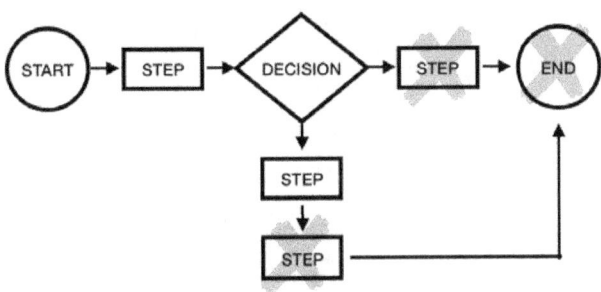

Left blank to draw the PROBLEMATIC Process Map.

STEP 3: DESIRED RESULTS

SMART Desired Results Checklist:

- ## For better focus, limit desired results to three or less.

Desired Result SMART Checklist (Complete this checklist for each desired result.) PROBLEM: _____		
Desired Result #3:	Yes	No
Is the desired result **Specific**?		
Is the desired result **Measurable**?		
Is the desired result **Achievable**?		
Is the desired result **Relevant**?		
Is the desired result **Time-Related**?		

Desired Result SMART Checklist (Complete this checklist for each desired result.) PROBLEM: _____		
Desired Result #3:	Yes	No
Is the desired result **Specific**?		
Is the desired result **Measurable**?		
Is the desired result **Achievable**?		
Is the desired result **Relevant**?		
Is the desired result **Time-Related**?		

Desired Result SMART Checklist (Complete this checklist for each desired result.) PROBLEM: _____		
Desired Result #3:	Yes	No
Is the desired result **Specific**?		
Is the desired result **Measurable**?		
Is the desired result **Achievable**?		
Is the desired result **Relevant**?		
Is the desired result **Time-Related**?		

Desired Results Summary

- Fill in the problem title, name of measure/metric on the first and second rows.
- Fill in the status of each checklist category.

Desired Results Summary
Problem: _____

Checklist	Measure / Metric #1	Measure / Metric #2	Measure / Metric #3
Current State Measurement as of Date: _____			
Desired State of Measurement			
Estimated Completion Date:			
Who is this relevant to?			
Status / Comments			

STEP 4: DETERMINE PROBLEM ROOT CAUSES

Ishikawa Diagram or Fishbone Analysis

- Write the problem title inside the arrow diagram.
- For the first level branches (thick line), come up with main reasons the problem is occurring. These will be your problem reason categories.
  - Common Problem Categories: People, Resources, Processes, Policies, Measurement, Environment
- Each branch level is a sub-cause of the previous one.
  - Ask the question *Why?* in relation to the previous level, not of the main problem.
  - The purpose of root cause analysis is to use deductive reasoning to reach a specific root cause.
    - It is a common misconception to put the next level answers in any branch.
- Work on each problem category one at a time.
- Add sub-branches as needed.
- The last branch level of each main category (dotted lines) contains the root causes.

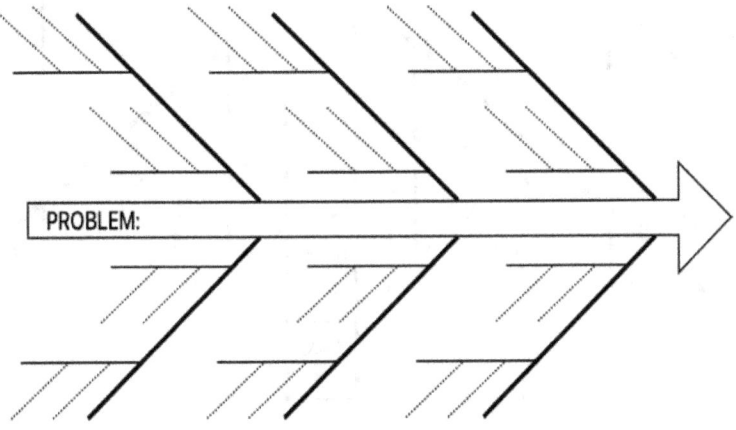

PROBLEM:

Larger version of Fishbone Diagram.

PROBLEM:

Five Why's Analysis

- Write down the problem title on top of your table.
- Write down at least five main categories as to why the problem is happening.
  - Common Problem Categories: People, Resources, Processes, Policies, Measurement, Environment
- Work on one main category at a time.
- For each main category, ask the question *Why?* until you get to the fifth *Why?*
  - At each level ask the question *Why?* of the previous level (not of the main level). Do this in order to use deductive reasoning to reach a more specific root cause.
- The fifth level answer to *Why?* below is printed in darker text to signify as root causes.

PROBLEM	
#1 WHY?	REASON 1
#2 WHY?	REASON 2
#3 WHY?	REASON 3
#4 WHY?	REASON 4
#5 WHY?	**REASON 5 - ROOT CAUSE**

Five Why's Analysis Table

FIVE WHY'S ANALYSIS PROBLEM:				
Category Reason 1	Category Reason 2	Category Reason 3	Category Reason 4	Category Reason 5
Level 1 Why?	Level 1 Why?	Level 1 Why?	Level 1 Why?	Level 1 Why?
Level 2 Why?	Level 2 Why?	Level 2 Why?	Level 2 Why?	Level 2 Why?
Level 3 Why?	Level 3 Why?	Level 3 Why?	Level 3 Why?	Level 3 Why?
Level 4 Why?	Level 4 Why?	Level 4 Why?	Level 4 Why?	Level 4 Why?
Level 5 Why? (Root Cause)	**Level 5 Why?** (Root Cause)	**Level 5 Why?** (Root Cause)	**Level 5 Why?** (Root Cause)	**Level 5 Why?** (Root Cause)

STEP 5: PRIORITIZE SOLUTIONS

Develop Solutions

- Refer back to previous step *Determine Problem Root Causes* and write down your root causes in the provided table below.
  - Write down root causes on the left gray side of the table. You do not need to list them in any order.
  - To the right side of each gray box, write down one to three *SMART* solutions for each root cause.
    - *Specific, Measurable, Achievable, Relevant, Time-related.*
      - Circle *Yes* or *No* on the provided table below.
    - Determine the impact of the solution to the overall problem.
      - Circle *Low, Med* or *Hi* on designated space.
    - Determine the amount of effort it would take to implement each solution.
      - When determining efforts, consider all resources such as time, money, and people.
      - Consider whether the resources you need to implement are within your control or not.
      - Solutions that require more resources and/or outside of your control would normally take more effort to implement.
      - Circle *Low, Med* or *Hi* on designated space.
  - Add additional rows if needed if you have more root causes than the table provided. Reminder to try to have ten or less to have better focused solutions.

List of Non-Prioritized *SMART* Solutions

#	Root Causes (Not Prioritized)	SMART Solution A	SMART Solution B (Optional)	SMART Solution C (Optional)
	LIST OF SMART SOLUTIONS **PROBLEM:** _____			
1		1A SMART: Yes No Impact: Low Med Hi Effort: Low Med Hi	1B SMART: Yes No Impact: Low Med Hi Effort: Low Med Hi	1C SMART: Yes No Impact: Low Med Hi Effort: Low Med Hi
2		2A SMART: Yes No Impact: Low Med Hi Effort: Low Med Hi	2B SMART: Yes No Impact: Low Med Hi Effort: Low Med Hi	2C SMART: Yes No Impact: Low Med Hi Effort: Low Med Hi
3		3A SMART: Yes No Impact: Low Med Hi Effort: Low Med Hi	3B SMART: Yes No Impact: Low Med Hi Effort: Low Med Hi	3C SMART: Yes No Impact: Low Med Hi Effort: Low Med Hi
4		4A SMART: Yes No Impact: Low Med Hi Effort: Low Med Hi	4B SMART: Yes No Impact: Low Med Hi Effort: Low Med Hi	4C SMART: Yes No Impact: Low Med Hi Effort: Low Med Hi
5		5A SMART: Yes No Impact: Low Med Hi Effort: Low Med Hi	5B SMART: Yes No Impact: Low Med Hi Effort: Low Med Hi	5C SMART: Yes No Impact: Low Med Hi Effort: Low Med Hi

List of Non-Prioritized *SMART* Solutions (Continued)

#	Root Causes (Not Prioritized)	SMART Solution A	SMART Solution B (Optional)	SMART Solution C (Optional)
6		6A SMART: Yes No Impact: Low Med Hi Effort: Low Med Hi	6B SMART: Yes No Impact: Low Med Hi Effort: Low Med Hi	6C SMART: Yes No Impact: Low Med Hi Effort: Low Med Hi
7		7A SMART: Yes No Impact: Low Med Hi Effort: Low Med Hi	7B SMART: Yes No Impact: Low Med Hi Effort: Low Med Hi	7C SMART: Yes No Impact: Low Med Hi Effort: Low Med Hi
8		8A SMART: Yes No Impact: Low Med Hi Effort: Low Med Hi	8B SMART: Yes No Impact: Low Med Hi Effort: Low Med Hi	8C SMART: Yes No Impact: Low Med Hi Effort: Low Med Hi
9		9A SMART: Yes No Impact: Low Med Hi Effort: Low Med Hi	9B SMART: Yes No Impact: Low Med Hi Effort: Low Med Hi	9C SMART: Yes No Impact: Low Med Hi Effort: Low Med Hi
10		10A SMART: Yes No Impact: Low Med Hi Effort: Low Med Hi	10B SMART: Yes No Impact: Low Med Hi Effort: Low Med Hi	10C SMART: Yes No Impact: Low Med Hi Effort: Low Med Hi

LIST OF SMART SOLUTIONS

PROBLEM: _____

Prioritize Solutions

- Use the *Prioritization Matrix* to prioritize the list of developed solutions.
  - Using the designated letters and numbers from the list of solutions, place them on the prioritization matrix based on effort needed to implement and impact to the problem.
  - A larger version of the matrix is provided next page if you would like to write out the solutions.
  - For simpler prioritization, use the four quadrants.
    - *Upper Left* = Low Effort, High Impact
      - Ideal Solutions
    - *Lower Left* = Low Effort, Low Impact
      - Less Suitable Solutions
    - *Upper Right* = High Effort, High Impact
      - May Need Business Case Analysis or Determination whether effort or investment is worth the gain of the impact.
    - *Lower Right* = High Effort, Low Impact
      - Least Suitable Solutions

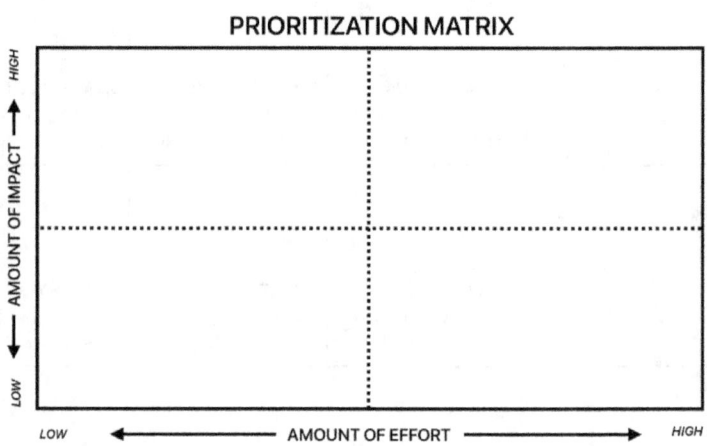

PRIORITIZATION MATRIX

Prioritization Matrix (Larger Version)

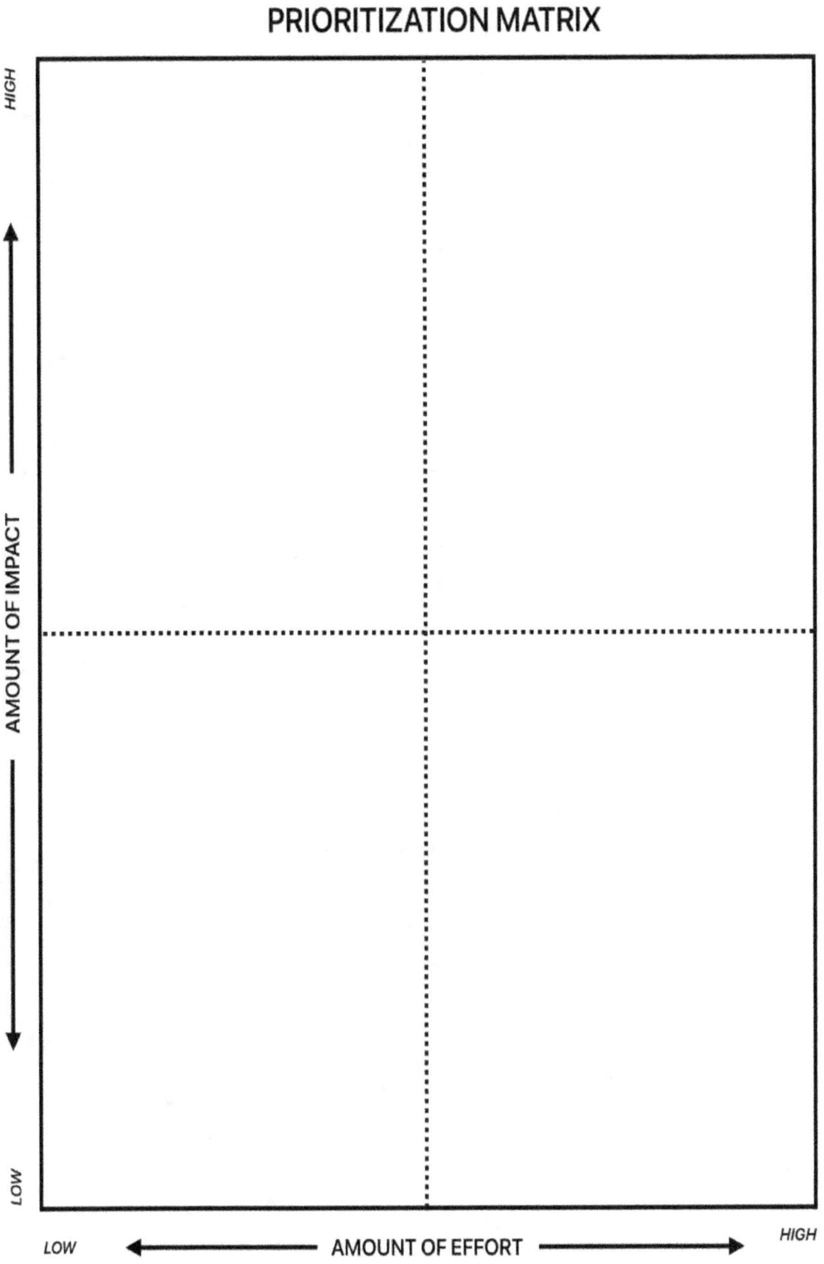

PRIORITIZATION MATRIX

HIGH

↑

AMOUNT OF IMPACT

↓

LOW

LOW ←————— **AMOUNT OF EFFORT** —————→ *HIGH*

Once all solutions are placed in the Prioritized Solution Matrix, re-list all the solutions in priority order.

Priority	Prioritized SMART Solutions	Estimated Completion Date	Root Cause(s) Affected
1			
2			
3			
4			
5			
6			
7			
8			
9			
10			

Prioritized Solution List (Continued)

Priority	Prioritized SMART Solutions	Estimated Completion Date	Root Cause(s) Affected
11			
12			
13			
14			
15			
16			
17			
18			
19			
20			

Prioritized Solution List (Continued)

Priority	Prioritized SMART Solutions	Estimated Completion Date	Root Cause(s) Affected
21			
22			
23			
24			
25			
26			
27			
28			
29			
30			

STEP 6: CHOSEN SOLUTIONS

Chosen Solutions

- Write the problem title.
- Choose no more than ten (10) solutions to implement.
  - If this is a personal project, start with one to five solutions to implement since you will not have other people to help.
- Keep the others on the list for future implementation.

CHOSEN PRIORITIZED SOLUTIONS

PROBLEM:

Priority #	Chosen Solution	Start Date	Estimated Completion Date	Point of Contact	Status / Comments
1					
2					
3					
4					

Chosen Solutions List (Continued)

CHOSEN PRIORITIZED SOLUTIONS
PROBLEM:

Priority #	Chosen Solution	Start Date	Estimated Completion Date	Point of Contact	Status / Comments
5					
6					
7					
8					
9					
10					

STEP 7: FOLLOW-UP

Follow-Up for Chosen Solutions

- Record your comments each time you do a follow-up.
- Follow-up at least monthly. Follow-up weekly if the estimated completion date is in three months or less.

FOLLOW-UP COMMENTS FOR CHOSEN PRIORITIZED SOLUTIONS

PROBLEM:

Priority #	Chosen Solution	Status / Comments
1		Entered by: _____ Date: _____
2		Entered by: _____ Date: _____
3		Entered by: _____ Date: _____
4		Entered by: _____ Date: _____

FOLLOW-UP FOR CHOSEN SOLUTIONS (Continued)

FOLLOW-UP COMMENTS FOR CHOSEN PRIORITIZED SOLUTIONS

PROBLEM:

Priority #	Chosen Solution	Status / Comments
5		Entered by: _____ Date: _____
6		Entered by: _____ Date: _____
7		Entered by: _____ Date: _____
8		Entered by: _____ Date: _____
9		Entered by: _____ Date: _____
10		Entered by: _____ Date: _____

Follow-Up for Desired Results

- Record your comments each time you do a follow-up.
- Follow-up at least monthly. Follow-up weekly if the estimated completion date is in three months or less.

FOLLOW-UP COMMENTS FOR CHOSEN PRIORITIZED SOLUTIONS PROBLEM:	
Desired Result	Status / Comments
	Entered by: _____ Date: _____
	Entered by: _____ Date: _____
	Entered by: _____ Date: _____

Visualization for Desired Results

- Plot results in the provided graph below for each follow-up; use one graph for each desired result.
  - For each graph, write the *Problem Title* on top.
  - Write the name of the *measure* for each desired result on the left side of the graph.
  - Fill in the number scale on the left side of the graph. Make sure to be consistent with increments.
  - Annotate the time measurement you are using on the bottom of the graph (i.e. minutes, hours, days, weeks, months, years)
  - Plot the ideal desired result measurement as a dotted line.
  - Plot the current result measurement as a solid line.
- Follow-up at least monthly. Follow-up weekly if the estimated completion date is within three months.
- Consider re-assessment if you don't see any improvement within 25% of the allotted project time.

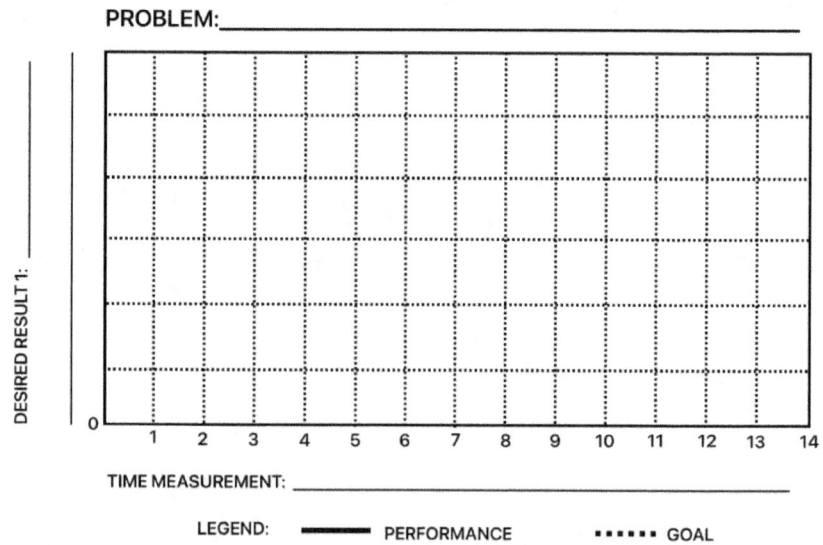

Visualization for Desired Results (Continued)

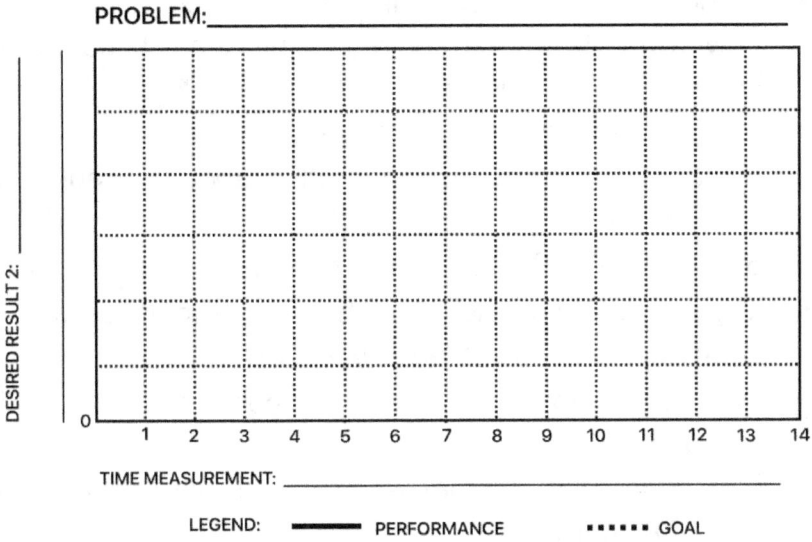

PROBLEM:_____

DESIRED RESULT 2:

0   1   2   3   4   5   6   7   8   9   10 11 12 13 14

TIME MEASUREMENT: _____

LEGEND: ▬▬▬ PERFORMANCE   ▪▪▪▪▪▪ GOAL

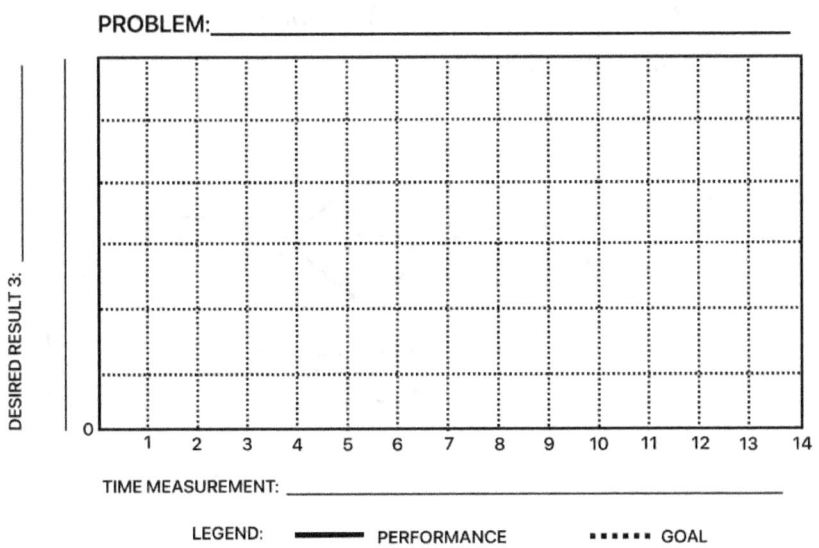

PROBLEM:_____

DESIRED RESULT 3:

0   1   2   3   4   5   6   7   8   9   10 11 12 13 14

TIME MEASUREMENT: _____

LEGEND: ▬▬▬ PERFORMANCE   ▪▪▪▪▪▪ GOAL

Visualization for Corrected Process

- Using the sample below draw the corrected process of how you get to each desired result; there should only be one process per A3.
  - *Circle* = Start and End of the process.
  - *Rectangle* = Process steps that does not require a decision.
  - *Diamond* = Process steps that require a decision.
- If you did not make any changes, simply draw the same process from *What is the Gap?* step.
- Annotate with an X any process that are still problematic.
  - Update the X marks as each step turn non-problematic.
  - Summarize what happened in comments under *Follow-Up Comments for Prioritized Chosen Solutions* or *Follow-Up Comments for Desired Results* or in your *Journal*.

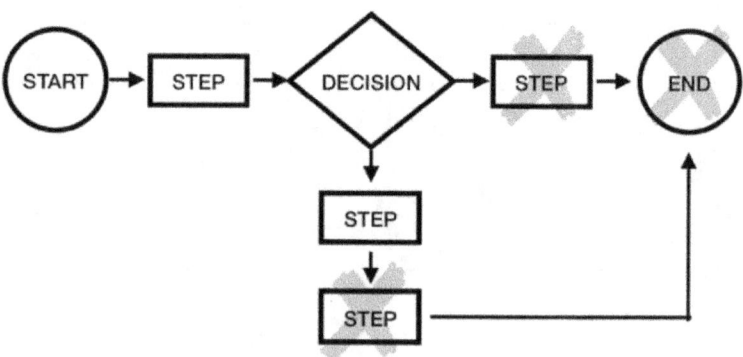

Left blank to draw the CORRECTED Process Map.

STEP 8: SUSTAINMENT

Follow-Up Dates for Chosen Solutions

- Continue Step 7, *Follow-Up*; record the dates below.
- Follow-up at least monthly. Follow-up weekly if the estimated completion date is in three months or less.

FOLLOW-UP DATES FOR CHOSEN SOLUTIONS

FOLLOW-UP DATES FOR CHOSEN SOLUTIONS														
PROBLEM:														
Chosen Solutions	Follow-Up Dates													
1.														
2.														
3.														
4.														
5.														

FOLLOW-UP DATES FOR CHOSEN SOLUTIONS (Continued)

FOLLOW-UP DATES FOR CHOSEN SOLUTIONS															
PROBLEM:															
Chosen Solutions					Follow-Up Dates										
6.															
7.															
8.															
9.															
10.															

Follow-Up Dates for Desired Results

- Continue Step 7, *Follow-Up*; record the dates below.
- Follow-up at least monthly. Follow-up weekly if the estimated completion date is in three months or less.

FOLLOW-UP DATES FOR CHOSEN SOLUTIONS
PROBLEM:

Desired Results							Follow-Up Dates								
1.															
2.															
3.															

turn Failure to Success choose to CHANGE

by Grace R. Devera-Montaño

THE JOURNAL

JOURNAL

- Journaling or documenting your change journey is important for the whole change process and especially for *Sustainment*.
- Documentation enables you to review thoughts, emotions, or any other things you have done during this change journey.
- You can also use the *Journal* portion of this workbook as an extension to any *Comments/Status* that does not fit in the provided tables.
- Journals do not have to be written words; use doodles, pictures, drawings as you see fit.
- At a minimum, create a journal entry each time you do a follow-up for *Chosen Solutions* and *Desired Results*.
- Date each journal entry.
- Enter the name of the person documenting the *Journal* entry, especially if conducting the change process for a group (i.e. family, team, organization).

Journal Entry

Entered by: _____   *Date:* _____

Journal Entry

Entered by: _____   *Date:* _____

Journal Entry

Entered by: _____   *Date:* _____

Journal Entry

Entered by: _____   *Date:* _____

Journal Entry

Entered by: _____   *Date:* _____

Journal Entry

Entered by: _____   *Date:* _____

Journal Entry

Entered by: _____   *Date:* _____

Journal Entry

Entered by: _____   *Date:* _____

Journal Entry

Entered by: _____   *Date:* _____

Journal Entry

Entered by: _____   *Date:* _____

Journal Entry

Entered by: _____   *Date:* _____

Journal Entry

Entered by: _____   *Date:* _____

Journal Entry

Entered by: _____   *Date:* _____

Journal Entry

Entered by: _____   *Date:* _____

Journal Entry

Entered by: _____   *Date:* _____

Journal Entry

Entered by: _____   *Date:* _____

Journal Entry

Entered by: _____   *Date:* _____

Journal Entry

Entered by: _____   *Date:* _____

Journal Entry

Entered by: _____   *Date:* _____

Journal Entry

Entered by: _____   *Date:* _____

ABOUT THE AUTHOR
Grace R. Devera-Montaño

Thank you for buying this book. Hopefully it serves you well.

I was born and raised in the Philippines. I finished High School in the United States. Not having funds for college, I enlisted in the United States Air Force (USAF) and made it a career. While in USAF I was privileged enough to finish my Bachelor's in Science in Psychology and Masters in Business Administration before retirement. After retiring from USAF, I found work as a civil servant for the United States Army.

I value and appreciate my faith in God and family. My husband and I met in the USAF and together we raised two beautiful and well-rounded children. I believe in lifetime learning. I also believe in giving back and helping others.

Just like many immigrants, I pride myself as a self-starter and resilient person. Having started my life in poverty in the Philippines, I am truly grateful for the opportunities United States has to offer.

I believe that anyone can succeed with the right mindset. No one is perfect and everyone has failed one way or another. I have had my shares of failures and thoughts of giving up. Some challenges are longer than others, but each time God eventually helps me realize that failure is nothing but a step in the learning process. I have learned from my church, that as long as I have faith in God, no matter what the outcome of my situation is, everything will be alright. So friends, don't give up. Choose to turn that failure to success.

www.ingramcontent.com/pod-product-compliance
Lightning Source LLC
Chambersburg PA
CBHW070749290526
45795CB00002B/542